TEMPEST

POEMS

Meyer, Ryan.
1st Edition.
ISBN: 978-0-578-83175-6
e-Book ISBN: 978-0-578-83176-3

Epigraph from "Prayers/Triangles" by Deftones, from *Gore* (2016)
John Ashbery quote in "Come Around" from "Yclept," in *Commotion of the Birds* (2016)

Cover & back cover designed by Ryan Meyer, via PicMonkey Photo Editor and Graphic Design Maker
Cover & back cover art – Photo by Stephane YAICH on Unsplash, @stefyaich
Author photo by Sarah Farrell, Magic Circle
Type set, and front and back type set in Times New Rowman

NothingPeak.com

TEMPEST

POEMS

RYAN MEYER

ALSO BY RYAN MEYER:

Haunt (2018)

FOREWORD

Tempest is a title I've always known I would give to a book of my poems. What it would consist of, and what messages it would contain, would be a different story. I think it perfectly captures the style I pour into a lot of my work, a blending of musical, rhythmic-sounding poetry that, when broken down and unraveled, reveals much darker, more vulnerable themes. I find the word "tempest" to be a word that sounds beautiful, but obviously represents something terrifying and destructive. It's a soft and arguably soothing word, paired with a meaning that opposes such a feeling. When I first heard the song "Tempest" by Deftones, on their *Koi No Yokan* album, I said to myself, "That's it. That's what I've been trying to capture in my work, a dichotomy that they've given us with this song." It's resonant throughout the whole album, really, but seeing that song title assured what I'd been trying to describe for some time.

With my first book, *Haunt*, I wasn't aiming to write about myself. Every piece was fictional. But I've learned that everything a writer or artist creates contains a piece of themselves, in some way. There are pieces in this collection much more personal to me, and I found it tough to think about publishing them for all to see. But there is a power to owning your vulnerabilities, and a definite growth through doing so. They've undeniably become strengths in this process. Of course, I've still got a long way to go, but I've come a long way in the last few years alone. I'm stronger now, and I'll speak for those involved in my life story by saying that they are stronger now, too. I look up to those people with the upmost respect, and I want them to know that. You know who you are.

This book is of course for poets and lovers of poetry, but also for the daydreamers, and those who are still figuring out who they are. I hope some of these words inspire someone out there to face their own tempest storm head-on.

~ Ryan

CONTENTS

"I PULL MY HEART OUT, BEWARE."
 - *DEFTONES*, "PRAYERS/TRIANGLES"

FLAMINGO

You're crowded by deadlines
And forged from pink flamingo sunsets
That call you on Friday nights
Just when you've opened the bottle of pinot
From that trip to Wine Country

Hazy-brained alkaline mind
Only as charged as your phone
Left unattended by the windowsill
Catching rays in rainbow glare,   dreaming
They could kiss your hair instead

The leaves on your potted plants
Softly graze your back
As you plank on the living room floor
Eyes closed: they're green palms waving
Your Tree Pose, spilled soil becomes
Sand between your toes

Outside, rush hour rolls high tide
Ebbing and flowing, and only
A blaring horn pulls you back to shore
Your surfboard cursor
Bobs along the surface

Gulls shriek the morning alarm on Monday
And your continental breakfast
Is dark roast in the pineapple mug
You got for your thirtieth

By three, sunlight reaches your desk
At the office, drapes along your hands
Halfway through the Big Weekly Task
You revel in the warmth

TWISTED ANKLES

Pry my fingers
Out of their fist
And see the
Underbelly
Of my palm,
Pale and lined
With the future.

It hasn't been easy,
Allowing myself
To see what
Lies ahead,
But at times
It's all I have.

If only
I could unzip them
And step through,
To just skip
The cobblestones
And bring me
To ground
Safe enough to
Take off my shoes.

I can't keep
Twisting my ankles
Over these rocks,
Smooth, but just
A bit too far apart.

Softer soil seems
So much farther away;
I hope it's worth
Keeping my feet

Protected
A bit longer.

SOMEWHERE ELSE

Sounds like a dream;
Like somewhere you'd only
Read about in a book,
Perhaps a distant place that
Sounds great on paper
But ends up just as
Disappointing as
Right Here.

CAN'T FLY FOREVER

My best is silence on a park bench,
        alone with my thoughts,
        fiddling with the paper that once
        wrapped my lunch.

Funny, how it can't be flattened
        out again, without blemishes, to
        the way it used to be.

I'm my best under spring skies,
        just before sunset, near
        a flock of birds that chose,
        for some reason, to land there.

They're content with that,
        with the decisions they've made,
        so I can be, too.

NO SCIENCE TO LONELINESS

Small, and light as a sparrow, the little one
Discovered the sudden stickiness of sap;
Something so common, so
Everyday… routine, even,
Grabbed him in its unclenching fist
And never let go.

His tail, adorned with feathers,
Was rendered immobile
And he, defenseless. Vulnerable
To the elements and any
Potential predator.
If only fate was merciful.

Certainly his thoughts raced,
Even *if* primal and lacking
A moral compass, or a sense
Of isolation. Who's to say?
It would be nice, if not
Heartbreaking,

Had he hoped
For another to find him?
Family, a friend to wander by
And help set him free?
What would be his next meal?
Could his last meal have been
Just that—his last?
His belly would surely grumble
At the thought.

The wind through the trees,
Combing their leaves,
Serves him a lullaby
For every night of

The rest of his life.

He is shaded from the sun,
So at least those with wings
Might not see him.
He does whimper though;
He has to. He worries what
Will become of him.

Will he be reduced to
Dust and bones? Will the sap
Harden and keep his little tail
For itself? Will anyone else
Remember him?

It would be nice to think
That at his last moment
He would lay his head down
On the soft earth
And let the wind sing him to sleep
One final time.

And let the amber that results
Be the only thing to honor him.

ON EVOLUTION

I organize and re-organize
My shelves too often.
Yearning for change,
Perhaps.

Songs are added to and removed
From playlists weekly;
Nothing can satisfy.
My ears ache for more,
Though I'm not sure what.

I often think:
What's it like living
An entire life as the caterpillar?

He's fine—no need to study him.
His fuzzy back is soft, and
He lives step by careful step.
He knows there is something
More he can be. Or at least,

He knows that he's spinning
His stringy capsule for a reason.

Am I building my cocoon?
Are all these big life plans
Just the start?

I hope growing wings
Doesn't have to hurt.

CAVERNOUS

Sweat leaves me
And bleeds through my sheets,
Making cold my back
In crude irony.

I traipse through
A forest of my own thoughts.
I hope a door lies at the end,
Held open so I can fall through.

Maybe the drop will snap me
Out of my sleepless reflections,
Or at least carry me to a light
That reflects my face back to me.

These are good times.
So why does my head still ache?
Why do my eyelids hang
Like stalactites,
Threatening closure?

Even my dreams leave me
An anxious mess, feeling as if
I've missed something, that I
Have reason to be worried.

Pieces have scattered
Beneath the couch; pieces to
A long-discarded puzzle. One day
I'll realize I don't need to
Spend time searching.

LONG, LONG AFTER

Kneeling on the grass, or what's left of it,
She hesitates to pluck the lone dandelion
From the ground. It flutters in the breeze,
As though shivering at the thought
Of no longer being rooted to the earth,

The way everything was
Before pie tins on the kitchen table
Became ashtrays beneath wrinkled faces
And split ends. Before car rides
With the windows down became
Transport between two
Opposite magnetic poles.

Hazy as it is, the light from the sun clings
To the flower's little white fluff...
Just as mom and pop should have
When they had it all.

She remembers chocolate milk
With extra syrup, and a curfew,
When the streetlights came on at night.
Her mother braiding her hair
In front of the big mirror,
Fashioning the ends with red bows.

Dusk approaches, absorbing the sky's blues
And leaving purples and browns behind.
She knows she could sit for hours
And return home regardless of the time.
Retreating her dirt-caked hands,
Knuckles cracked and worn,
She does not pick the dandelion. Instead,
She stands and brushes herself off
And heads home.

THRESHOLD

We approach the place where they say Death resides
In every gap, along every surface.
A legend whose existence we had to challenge.

We have our doubts, but as we approach,
We can feel a growing sense of dread.
Almost as if we've reached the edge of the world,
All color disappears; the texture of the earth
Is riddled with cracks and imperfections,
Blemishes and mistakes.

Death cannot be fixed. Not completely.

My friend looks at me, hopelessness
Filling his stare. We were told not to let this place
Get to us. No thoughts should be allowed
Past the forefront; nothing could be dwelled upon.

Yet, I think about my mother, around whom
Death could never secure his bony grip.
My grandfather, who seemed to slip, suddenly,
Right through his fingers.
My cousin, who stumbled, and couldn't
Find the means to make it out of Death's clutch,
No matter how hard he tried.

An End being so close, just a single step away,
Makes time slow, but not exactly to a stop.
Gravity feels sparse—I swim in an ocean without water.
My friend turns away; tears stream from his eyes.
He crumbles down onto all fours, completely distraught
With grief. This place, on the cusp of emptiness,
Is the embodiment of ambient sound.

It makes me yearn for life's monotony, because

Even that is something more. I want to scrub
Clean the bathtub in my childhood home—the one
Of black porcelain that hid away all traces of dirt.
I wish I could listen to the stories of an old
Family friend, whose name I can never remember,
And whose stories I immediately forget.
I ache for my daily hour-long commute to work,
Where the minutes waste away
Like the Valentine's Day roses on my desk.
I'm lucky if I can keep them alive for a week.

This place can't keep me alive
For ten seconds, if I choose to cross the threshold.

I help my friend up and flee this place.
He wipes his tears away, but mine still linger on my cheeks,
Having snuck there without warning. I leave them there
To dry.

GIANT

My friend lights up on the front porch
And we stand in silence for a few moments
Before we start talking about the future
In lowered voices
As though it's a quiet giant,
Standing off in the dark
Just beyond the glow of the streetlamps,

Who we imagine has résumé paper skin
And a gut-full of jumped conclusions; maybe
It lumbers like three o'clock on a Tuesday
On feet made of wood and stone from
Unfinished projects around the house,

Who thinks with a mind
With too many tabs open, and constantly
Misses the train of thought,

Who we don't want to disturb
Lest they're easily upset, but who
We'd only wish the best for, and

Maybe
Offer a drag to.

GIANT, PART 2

They politely decline;
Our friend doesn't smoke,

But they step out of the dark,
Bathed in streetlamp sepia glow,
Revealing glassy skin that reflects us
Back to ourselves,

Only slightly distorted,
Small in size against a backdrop
Of such a big world

And a nonthreatening future
That is ever changing.

ANTLERS

Home wasn't built
For the antlers on my head,
Protruding from my skull
Like antennae—
Tangible headaches.
They scrape against
The ceiling and leave marks
In the plaster.
Unless it's a popcorn ceiling,
I trail shame behind me
With every step.
New limbs branch off
With every birthday,
A reminder that things
Only get more complicated
As time passes.
I'll just have to learn and
Re-learn to balance.

THAT DARK

Alone and finally focused, vulnerable,
You dance with the canvas
As love pours through the brush
In reds and yellows,
But pain follows, as always.
Black and the deepest blue,
Filling upturned eyes, nestled upon
Dark bags beneath, and those
Frown lines that curve 'round lips.
They're not anyone you know:
They're everyone you know.
They live in passersby, in coworkers,
In friends and neighbors, family.
They reside in your dreams,
Fictional, only based off
The interactions you lose sleep over.
So you fill the backdrop
With not a single ray of light,
So anything could live in that dark.
Even something worth waiting for.

A MELANCHOLY ALBUM COVER FOR THE COFFEE SHOP ARTIST

Find it at your local brew;
If your mind goes right to beer,
That's roughly the same audience.
Picture a washed-out image
Of a window blanketed by
White curtains and soft sunlight.
A notebook, long scribbled in,
Rests on the bedside table,
Ready for its photo shoot.
Or, sit in a wooden chair
And rest your head in your palm.
Let your fingers search through
Your hair, like they're looking for
The right chords to play
For your ex in the crowd
Congregating in someone's basement.
Croon about lost love,
Like you've lived a life of pain and hurt
In a short twenty-two years.
Dye your hair bleach blond
And pierce your nose.
Your voice is breathy, but soothing,
Although your range is frankly short,
But you're accessible. Relatable.
You're improving every day.
And sometimes, I can hear it
In your voice: you're a misty,
Empty forest, probably not far
From your own backyard.
The trees still wait for something
Worth shaking their leaves.

FAULTY WIRING

Mom was having another one of her fits
But this time she didn't have the chance
To make it to the couch or a bed.
There wasn't any blood; it wasn't like that
But her hands were cramped and her
Back was arched, convex, and
I could tell she was trying to fight it.
Her eyes were still hers, but her body
Became a machine with faulty wiring.

My grandmother's blue carpet centered the room;
There was the bed that creaked something wicked
No matter how you sat on it;
The TV on the bureau that has played
Every TBS and Lifetime sitcom;
The books and boxes of tissues stacked on the
Bedside table along with enough framed photographs
Of her grandchildren to fill an album.

But Mom still lay on the floor, twitching and
Fighting the tense muscles with forced grunts.
I called for help, but no one,
Not even my grandmother was
Anywhere to be found.
Maybe they were downstairs.
They wouldn't be able to hear me.
I tried to hold her hand like I always do,
More comforting for me than anything.
I watched those eyes that knew
What was happening, attached to
A brain that didn't.

My calls didn't echo down the stairs
Or out the open window, where the draft
Entered, slowly rocking the door behind me.

LAST FEW

Memories whirr around my head
Like gnats on a humid night;
They know about the car
Swerving along the road, they know
That they must work hard
In these next few—
These last few moments.

They gave me the first time
He held my hand; we were driving
With the top down on our first date,
To a place that didn't accept
Reservations. The wait was too long.
His hand was worn, but warm, and soft.

What soon followed was my first heartbreak,
On a night I knew would come
But could hardly face; I remembered
Feeling like it was the hardest thing
To endure, and man, was I wrong.

The gnats gave me getting buzzed
With a friend and stealing
An old traffic cone from someone's yard.
We made fun of ourselves all night.

A glimpse of hope passed through
In the form of family, friends,
Gathered together in the summer
While the dog scrambled around,
Too excited to contain herself.
Her spunk was uplifting, awe-inspiring;
A breath of fresh air in a polluted world.

I received drunkenly singing along

To the wrong Wham! song in public,
That memory is still a bit fuzzy.

They gave me countless nights
Of tears dampening my pillows, worried
Too much about what others thought.
To focus on happiness is hard
When you're someone who needs
Those around them to be happy.

I got more sadness than I'd wanted,
In those last few moments, but
The light at the end of the tunnel
Was just a pair of headlights
Reminding me that better times
Were just around the corner.

APRIL

Spring came late this year;
        or at least it was carried in
on the backs of chilly breezes
and nestled itself onto naked branches.

It didn't keep the birds away, though.
They still greeted us every morning
with welcoming songs of sunshine and dew;
        I should have appreciated them more
when we could all go out and join them.

A scary feeling is the future, written
in invisible ink, on pages with blank faces.
Each day blends together—ink blots
        made indecipherable, the dark
taking up far too much space.
Irony mimics the sound of the birds.

We took walks daily (at first), both
hoping to see more neighbors to
share smiles with, and wishing they'd
        keep their distance.

I write this in past-tense, hoping that
not too long from now, it won't be
considered more than wishful thinking.

REASSURANCE

I tried to be human
On a Sunday afternoon at home
In the bathroom while the 'rents were away.
The sunlight from the window touched my skin,
Soft, warning me not to be reckless.
I merely insisted that I
Was in the midst of reassurance.
The tub's tepid water was
Only slightly hazy from my haphazard cleaning.
Something about scrubbing down the smooth
White acrylic felt like I was wiping out
The insides of my skull, erasing
All the caked-on privilege,
The ignorance, and the selfish thoughts
That skated about like whispering imps.
My fingers skated, too, atop the water
As it ebbed and flowed, waiting
For someone to embrace.
Wanting to think no further,
I plunged my head beneath the surface
And listened to the pulsing of blood
Through my ears, the steady thudding
Of my heart in my head
As it fought to keep my lungs from
Flooding themselves with lukewarm tap water.
In those few moments, before I resurfaced,
I could finally hear myself

IS EVERYTHING OK?

The Wi-Fi doesn't work like it used to,
and my Aries has been surfacing
More frequently than ever.
It's not "inner," anymore—it barely classifies
As skin-deep.

The skies seem to want to shower us a lot.
Either they're really sad or we have
A lot of cleansing to do.
Can I pet the clouds like dogs?
Give them belly-rubs?
Maybe they're more like cats—
A pat on the head will suffice.

I've been writing things down a lot more lately,
Sometimes more than once.
Remind me to write a note to myself
To remind myself to write that down, alright?

Everything is going so well... so why
Do my gears still grind out headaches?
They're love poems I can't fall in love with.
Scraps of paper that take too long to dissolve into the dirt.

Even though I'm easily startled regardless,
I wish my thoughts would knock before entering.

Sorry, sadness isn't here, he's on his lunch break—

But hope is in her office.
She's been waiting for you.

SISYPHUS

I was merely a man.
I didn't realize how important it was to die
Until it was impossible to do so.

After taking lives and making threats,
Living a life of vanity and egoism,
I was to pay for my wrongdoings, but no,
I had to capture my captor and make matters worse.

With Hades locked in my closet, I watched
Men being pierced with blades without
As much as a drop of blood to show for it.
Years of deceit, of circling above the heads
Of men until they performed my bidding
Led to what I saw as that downfall of humanity.
They threw themselves
From cliff sides, only for the tide to
Wash them back ashore, air still
Swirling through their lungs.

Often I wondered how demoralizing it was
To be the King of the Underworld, handcuffed
And left in some knave's wardrobe
With only wooden sandals and several
Fluttering moths to accompany him.
When his skeletal knights kicked in my door
And set him free, I'd never felt closer to death.

My blood ran cold, yet the devil perched
On my shoulder wouldn't let me stop speaking
In my native tongue of manipulation.
I'd tricked once, and I'd trick again
Until all my responsibilities were evaded,
Until I was sure I was safe. In hindsight,
Assurance was never carved in stone.

There was a period of time before
The knights returned to my dwelling,
A few weeks' time that allowed me to think
About who I was and what I would become.
Where could a life of lies take me,
Other than below the ground I walked upon?
The Underworld left me alone for a while.
I imagined travelling the world, summiting
Mountains, watching the world beneath me
Carry on as though life itself
Hadn't gotten in the way of seeing
What lay beyond. I imagined living as a god,
But it seemed as though life had blinded me, as well.

Now I push against this weight
That keeps me from the peak of this rugged path
Where I will remain for eternity.
I see the vultures waiting with
A gleam of hunger in their eyes,
And I see through my hunger for power,

A vulture myself
I've become.

WAITING

Full of daydreams
And unfinished projects,
I fill in the answers
And forge the signatures
Of so many before me
To allow myself
To feel truly happy again.

Pin-pricks etch their way
Across my skin,
Skating along like bugs
With long legs;
Nothing but limbs.

I feel them when I sit still,
When my thoughts float,
Trapped against
My skull, clouds of
Anxious worries
And broken ideas.

I sent in the application
A few weeks ago.
I'm looking forward to
Feeling my cheeks flush
With color, and not
Being plagued with fatigue,
But I have yet
To hear back.

ODE

Beyond the trees,
The stars become lights
In the windows
Of apartment complexes.

Across babbling brooks,
Grasses sway and give way
To streetlamps and highways.

Past this wildlife,
Civilization mends
Its wounds, or tries to,
In green-colored plastic.

Only camera phones
Truly see the leaves
On their branches;
Zoom in on veins
That need no adrenaline.

They die bloodless
And silent, making dry
The throat of the earth.

We, however,
Do not, but
Our knees are felled
In the same sad fashion.

LUNCH BREAK

Caught up in work, I forget again about
The orange on my desk; It's lasted longer
Than I thought it would, but now it's going
Green in places, soft in others.

My fingers kiss the letters on the keyboard;
My eyes absorb the monitor's light.
The succulents on the shelf above
Are soldiering on—Larry and Curly. Moe didn't make it.
Guess I'm not responsible enough for plants.

While I look for that document,
For the third time this morning,
I'm distracted by the string lights I hung up
On the bookshelf behind my chair.
They aren't very bright, but they still pull me away
At the right times, reminding me
To take a breath.

I have accomplished a lot,
But with the New Year approaching
Like a blind wolf, I'm a bleeding rabbit
Who's just trying to find somewhere nice to lay
Before it finds me. I'll look up at the sky
One last time, hoping I appreciated the garden
Without focusing entirely on its roots.

CICADA

You have a tattoo
Of a cicada on your left forearm,
Styled with thick outlines
And faded shades of brown and green.
It's visible as you drink lukewarm coffee
From your favorite mug, the one
That might as well be for soup.
You have to hold it with both hands.

Most of us stare
At our phones at the table, but you
Stare out the window, eyes
Fixed on a spot along the brick wall
Of the building across the street.

I wonder what you're thinking:
Probably something work-related,
Or maybe about your brother-in-law
And his shitty attitude.
We've all got something going on.

All I can focus on is your demeanor,
Soft but sure, contemplative but rested.
I envy your cool; I covet your perception.

Your tousled hair, recently slept on,
Catches the morning sun; you push
Your glasses further up on the bridge
Of your nose, notice my stare,
And smile.

SANK

I push off
from the ocean floor
and float
towards the surface
with nothing more
than the hope
that the sun
will still be shining
when I get there.

There's no easy way to say this,
But your smile warms my heart.
It's contagious enough to curl my lips
Longer than they have on their own.
Your calm is relaxing. I find peace with you.
I want to drive with you,
With the top down,
With the music loud,
With your hand in mine, resting on my lap.
Our differences make me wary
To plan next steps, as though you've given me
A light bulb to screw into a lamp
Across a dark room. I try not to stumble.
I just don't want to break it. But I know it works.
I sigh like the wind with you—in long,
Heaving breaths that expel all my fears.
I'm still young. I care too much
About what others will think.
But looking at you, being with you,
I tell myself it doesn't matter.
Right now, nothing will replace
The warmth that you share with me.

There's no easy way to say this;
The words are hard to find, for
You leave me speechless.

FULL

I lay, sleepless,
Surrounded by rattling walls
Shaken by thunder.
The earth soaks up the rain,
Becomes soft,
Consumes the floor.
Mud seeps through,
Soon enough
Staining the sheets
And stinging my skin
Cold. I don't move.
There's no use.
The room becomes full
Of wasted summers
And sour conversations,
Dreams unrealized, and
Tears uncried. Tears
I wish I could drink up
To restore all I'd lost
Due to wasted breath
And silent anger.
Now I can float atop it,
And I can finally
Touch the ceiling,
But is it worth all the mess?

UNSTEADY

Hot summers were mouths
That molded us into wads
Of paper and spit, sending us
Soaring across the fields
At the edge of town.
It was her favorite place,
Somewhere we could get away,
Where only the nearby forest
Could hear us.

Neither of us knew
What we were doing;
We were young: fooling around,
Downing cheap vodka,
And smoking stale cigarettes
From our mothers' purses.

The tree deep in the woods
Where I lost my virginity to her
Still stands there, a monument
With deformed arms that wave
With the slightest breeze.
I never thought it could possibly
Be waving goodbye.

It was bound to happen, finding out
That she'd moved on. She told me
From the passenger seat of my first car,
A banged-up sedan I'd found at a junkyard.
And I remembered how we'd met,
Secluded in a closet at one of her girlfriends'
Sweaty house parties. That alone screams
"How can this last?"
She admitted she never thought it would.
She admitted she thought I was naïve.

But the river by the train tracks,
In full view of that waving tree,
Still babbles secrets along the brook.
Sometimes I'll sit nearby and listen to it echo
The confidences we'd shared
Amongst the brush, as we
Brushed skin to the most
Unsteady rhythms.

SOME THINGS YOU CAN'T UNDO

Peeling her shadow from the wall
Was easier done than I'd thought.
Like the clearance sticker
On a bargain-priced novel,
The outline of her frame slid
Cleanly from the plaster
And left not a mark on the blank space.
It lay limp in my palms,
No foundation to cling to,
And it felt like velvet draped
Across my fingers.
When I looked at her, shadow-less,
I saw a girl faded from reality
Blurred against the backdrop
Of her near-empty living room
With bare wood floors
And thick beige curtains
Open just enough to let in light,
But only a little.

THE WIND TRIES, TOO

It's never as graceful as it is in the movies.
Just before he stepped into the nothingness
Beyond the ledge at the top of his shabby
Apartment complex, his right knee buckled,
But his face didn't change a bit. He'd lived
In that building for three months after the fire
Took his family, his paintings, the bed
That he told me he'd lost his virginity on
In the seventh grade. I never believed him,
But it was easiest to let him think I did.

Homework in hand, I crinkled the pages
Of pencil-scribbled Algebra II answers,
Eyes glued to him, feet glued to the sidewalk
Right outside the building.
He needed to look over my answers, so
I told him I could come by. He needed help,
And I always showed all of my work. I think
I let go of them later; but I vaguely
Remember the unevenly torn pieces flying away.

A nail in this coffin, the sun shone
The brightest it had in weeks, following
Too many days of rain, as though it opened
Up the skies just for him. There were others
Walking past the building, trying to scoot around me,
Whispering hushed '*oops, sorry*'s and making sure
Their skin didn't brush against mine. If any of them saw,
Their reactions were much too late. Only I
Saw the descent, only I felt the silence,
Caged up in my lungs like a pet bird with clipped wings.

Plus, I think I saw a bit of myself in him,
Watching as the air did all it could
To keep his body up there, pulling by

The cuffs of his jeans, the knots in his hair.
I saw a boy trying to fly away, too.
His collared shirt, unbuttoned, billowed
Behind him as he fell. He looked like Superman
At the end of every movie, colliding with Earth
Only to be restored again just before the end credits.

EXISTENTIAL

After everything
we'd tried,
the only action
our robot could
perform
was to look
up at the stars
and sigh.

BITING

I'm unable to listen to myself:
I've been chewing at
The inside of my right cheek
For months, maybe a year,
At this point, and now
My jaw hurts at times.
Even more infrequently,
It'll crack, as if it's telling me
To lay off the anxious habit
Of trying to wipe
A previously blank slate clean.
The skin there needs to heal
On its own, but my tongue
Pokes and prods like a child
Armed with a stick,
Eyes locked on the tired slug
Cornered against a curb.
The irony is, I'm chewing
As I write these words,
A testament to my own
Stubbornness, shrunken
In the shadow of everything
Piled onto my shoulders,
An imperfect balancing act
During which, hopefully,
Nothing will come crashing down.

BOUQUET CHEEKS

It took you so long
To realize you loved her
That the rest of us
Wore constant smiles
As you both held hands
In front of us at your party.
You even switched
Your cigarette hand
So you could walk around
On her right side,
And if that wasn't real love,
We didn't know
What else was.
Plus, we could swear
You walked with a spring
In your step, and your cheeks
Were rosier than ever—
A full bouquet.

WE ALWAYS SAY WE'LL STAY IN TOUCH

Every cigarette I pull
Out of the bent pack in my pocket
Reminds me of you. I remember saying
Every other week that I planned
On quitting. How naïve – as though
We didn't go through like four packs
Of those on a good day, when your folks
Were out of town for their meetings.

Every ashtray in our wake was full
Of summers wasted at the canal
At the edge of town. It was near the spot
Where Jimmy had just barely found
The space between the wheels
Of the northbound freight and its tracks.
He was pretty shaken up, but once
We offered him a beer he calmed down.
It's funny, the things we find ourselves
Laughing about after some time.

I hear the canal is all dried up now,
But that was bound to happen,
Since all that was left when we were kids
Was about a foot of water, tops.
One of us nearly managed to drown
In that drainage; probably either of the twins.
They always showed up with trouble to cause,
So I guess that was bound to happen, too.
It's gross, to think of what must have been
Left behind in that water from the soles
Of our canvas sneakers. Water-logged
Cigarette butts, the occasional used condom,
When someone would sneak out with a girl…
And God-knows what else.

The time when Tim got caught
With weed in his car keeps coming
To mind. I can't believe how lucky he was
That his sister's boyfriend was a cop
Who could never pass up a hit.
You know that drop-off right past
The train tracks? Where we'd dangle our legs
And throw our voices like paper planes?
My mom said it used to be
Part of the old river that ran through town.
That's where we went after we convinced your brother
To buy us alcohol from the corner-store.
We must have crushed like twenty-four beers
Between us, man. Every "Do Not Litter" sign
Erected marked one of our spots,
A tongue-in-cheek game of capture the flag.
We were such idiots,
But I wouldn't trade it for the world.

Mom told me you were out of rehab-
That's why I'm writing. I know she saw us
As a bunch of delinquents with nothing
Ahead of us, but she always worried about you
As though you were one of her own.
She could tell things weren't going well for you,
And in hindsight, I should have told her.
I guess I thought we were invincible,
That I could keep you safe, somehow.

I think of you during my morning commutes to work,
As I pass by liquor stores
And abandoned skate parks.
When I listen to stories of adolescence
From the people I interview for the paper,
I can hear your embarrassing laugh.

I'm sorry we haven't spoken much;

Distance does something to your mind, dude,
I can't really explain it.
But go back to the drop-off, for me,
And shout into the wind. Let it all out.
You have no idea how badly I wish I could.

ALL YOUR FIRES

We wear gas masks
To prevent ourselves
From breathing in
The fumes from
All your fires, but
We never think to
Try and stop them
Before they spark.

DANDELION

We lay
Ageless
In a field
Of grass
That tickles
Our palms

Smiles
Catch
The sun
And hold it
In lips like
Hammocks

These winds
Whisper
Secrets
We cannot
Translate

They sound
Like time
And the fear
Of the
Future, silent,
That watches

LOVE

you don't want to pick up a stick
and poke the dead slug
off the path through the woods

you don't want to imagine
how it died, how it got there,
a creature that only knows what it knows
and no further

you don't want to know all about
this tiny spotted beast, but,
with that branch in your grip
and being only inches away from something new,

you do anyway.

THE POET

"This is not going to be a sad poem,"
He says, just before letting his mind wander.
Of course it's not, not at first.
But too many thoughts surface at once,
Like they always do, and then he worries
About being one of those depressing poets
Who writes about nothing but
Whiskey and cigarettes, whose napkins
Are all scribbled on with words
That echo love and loss, fear and longing,
Feelings he's not sure he completely understands.
Plus, he doesn't smoke, and he hates whiskey.

He wants to write the next Big Musing,
Or the Prize-Winning Piece, that
Twenty-Page-Long Stream-Of-Consciousness.
But worry and dread surface; existential
Ideas that buzz around in his head,
Bumping up against his skull
Like flies to a bug zapper.
Or, maybe he's the fly, and sad poems
Are the blue light he's so attracted to.
They're the person he writes about,
The lover that might not even exist,
The dark color of his coffee. No milk.
It upsets his stomach.

Regardless, he writes, and whatever
Words spill out from his palms he
Catches with his fingertips
So they can fill sentences.
He's going to hate them, at first.
He's going to put them away
For weeks, maybe months at a time,
And forget about them. They're too sad.

Maybe in the time that passes
He'll meet someone. He'll find that job
That he'll actually be happy with,
Or at least be content commuting to
Every day. He'll prove himself wrong.
He'll take some chances. He'll say "no."
He'll disappoint some people, hell,
He'll do it and he will get over it. He's
Got a life to live, a life that finally
Hits the ground running.

Maybe that will bring him back to
The discarded poems collecting dust,
Those boxes in the attic
That only contain chunky Christmas lights
He should have replaced ages ago.
By now the poems have yellowed
With time, as though they'd been created
Decades ago. He'll glance
Through them, skimming the words
As though he still knows them
And calls them every week
To check up and see how they've been.

They're not the same poems
That they were months ago;
They've aged, succumbed to erosion.
So when he digs through them
And finds that glimmer of gold,
Before he brushes it off, he stops.
He looks at the mug of coffee next to him,
Permanently stained from use,
Chipped in too many places. He stands up,
Brings it into the kitchen,
And adds a bit of milk and sugar.

BLOOM

I've walked in your garden
And dug up your weeds.
All I have to show for it are
Dirt-crusted hands and
Fistfuls of dead plants.
Their roots dangle,
With no life to give
And nothing to absorb.
Horrors are hidden
To allow blooming beauty
And fruitful crops.
Nothing extravagant;
Tomatoes, cucumbers,
Maybe lettuce. Some herbs.
But nothing here can grow
Without burying
Something else.

LIKE CEMENT

You feel as though you've gone grey

It enters through the ears first,
And fills your mind before
Becoming a permanent lump
In your throat

A constant cry threatens to burst,
But the rest pours into your lungs
And slows every breath

You feel as though you've gone grey

It seeps into your veins,
Clogs your nerves, numbs your limbs

Sluggish and faded, your
Daily routine seems forged
From a broken record, with no one
To help you move the needle

You feel as though you've   gone   grey

YOUNG ADULT

Full-bellied and
Ready to take on
The world,

We find nothing
Better than to
Drive with the
Windows down,
Going nowhere
In particular

To do next to
Nothing, and to
Have a damn
Good time

Doing it.

WEEDS

Let's bask in the sun that's left,
Even as our leaves dry out.
And as the fog rolls in,
We wait until it passes
In silent suspense.
Like cats, we brush up
Against your legs
As a sign of peace,
Hoping, with nerves rooted,
That you'll keep your flames
At bay.

SLANT

The frayed ends of severed ties
Blow in the wind like banners;
I use the tip of my tongue
As a diving board, but my posture
Is far from up-right.
The columns that support me
Have withered like flowers
Whose stems are bending
Beneath them.

Everything is leaning
Like a water bottle
With a crumpled bottom.
Diagonal lines seem to be
The norm around here,
Not uncommon, but my eyes
Constantly want to correct things.
They are hypocrites and my lungs
Are asking too much of me,
Especially when the dashboard
Illuminates my face and I sit
In the passenger seat, just trying
To get away from it all.

I can't be a marble column
With no foundation at my feet;
The soil beneath me is soft as it is,
And the rain hasn't stopped
For months.

COUGHING FITS

We choke on
misplaced lip balm
  as we search beneath car
seats

and expectations
  that exist only to let us
down

and sweaty palms
  from nervous thoughts that
haunt

and our parents
  who we fear letting down

and old habits
  that sting nostalgic

and anything intangible
  like love or anger or grief
or hope

and thumb tacks
  that we dropped months
ago and never found

and public lands
  that we drive through,
  pollute, disturb, disrespect

and private ones
  where we hide our demons,
buried deep in backyards

and cracked knuckles
        toes, ankles, wrists, elbows,
knees

and our passions
        that end up dragging us,
        bloodied and bruised, down
        busy streets

and our tears
        that come to us when we
        need them most, or even
        just when we lay in bed at
        night, restless, staring at the
        ceiling, not knowing for
        sure

what we're feeling.

CULTURE SHOCK

Strangers made familiar
make what has become "love"
in a place too public
for decency for me to still feel
the need to hang around;

these pulsing lights make this
a dreamscape all too real.

Bad attempts to pick-up
stick to me like shrink wrap,
threatening to stay too long.
Pride has evolved,

and I'm not seasoned enough
to critique this meal.

Some of us still quiver
behind closet doors, afraid
of ourselves, unsure of
what lies beyond.
Pills and lines lead them
to a world of self-loathing
and a hierarchy
that feels too familiar

and not as colorful
as one might think.

Maybe it's pessimistic,
considering new challenges
are made,

while others
are finally won.

STOP, HOLD, RELEASE

Been dying for a revelation
To descend from the clouds
And catch me in its talons.
Hope the wind can pull
All the breath from my lungs.
Force me to stop, hold, and
Release all of the built-up bad.
Spit it towards the sky, like
A wad of paper through a straw.
Dream of the grass when I'm
Finally lowered to the ground,
Blades poking between my fingers
To peer above my knuckles
And make sure that I'm okay.
Whisper to them that no, maybe
Not right now, but this far along,
I think I will be.

IMPERFECT FIT

I portray my thoughts with shadow puppets
As the light flickers against the walls.

You lean in closely to tell me they don't make sense
So I can finally understand that nothing ever will.

The shadow rabbit with the crooked ears cocks his head
To show me that he's sympathetic, but minimally,

And it's not clear along the plaster, but he bends
Over and begins to remove his insides so he can

Stare at them, splayed out along the floor
Like a grisly jigsaw puzzle in which the pieces

Don't fit cleanly back together

I'M SORRY

but I can't
be sorry
anymore.

COME AROUND

"The past should be more confident.
It has little to lose, and everything to gain."
John Ashbery, "Yclept"

Almost two years in,
After many nights of tear-stained pillows
And impenetrable arguments,
We brought a fruit platter to the party.
It was hot, that July… or was it August?
Nerves nestled on a bed of open arms.

And later, we all attended your birthday,
Piled in the car, totally out of left field,
But normalcy usually is, is it not?
Like there was nothing to worry about;
Still, it must have felt like a leap of faith
You didn't think you were ready for.

Looking back, it's funny to think
About the women who wouldn't have
Let this go any other way, who stood,
Arms crossed, one foot tapping,
Eyes staring daggers, unmovable,
In the way of all other outcomes.

Now, at weekly Sunday dinners,
With too much food for this amount of people
(Which you once teased your mother-in-law about),
You know a six pack and a bottle of chardonnay
Are just enough for the right gift basket,

Especially with your hand always there
For support, underneath.

STRAIGHT Bs

I

These winds haven't picked up much, yet,
But the leaves dance across the pavement
And scrape tambourine sounds of a beat
For the branches above to shimmy to.
They beckon me out into the open,
To locally-owned coffee shops,
Bars full of high school acquaintances,
And city lounges with pretty socialites
Seemingly on tap.

Glances shy away on the forbidden faces
Of men who seem to have it all together,
Women awaiting introductions, and
People skating across and between
Who have much, much more to fear
Than I do. Yet they bare their labels,
If they're comfortable enough.

Before you've "picked," your letter
Isn't yet carved into your forearm
For the rest of the spectrum to see. Like
Receiving the wrong grade on a test,
Time and time and time again;
It's tough to seamlessly mold
An "F" into an "A," when passing
Is just so far out of reach.

II

The last of the sun's rays
Peer from behind storm clouds
That billow along the floor
Of this relatively empty dais.

I can exit stage left or right,
But both options are wrong.

Still, the lights guide me,
Inch by inch, to the dance floor,
Where glances have evolved
Into lower back rubs
And playful smiles with averted eyes.
Everyone's hair is dewy with sweat,
Glistening beneath prismatic glow.
It's dim enough for anyone
To be a dance partner.

If only our letters
Could glow in the dark.

III

Outside, the air has cooled
And is tinged with specks of rain.
Whistling gusts lead me along the sidewalk,
Anywhere from here.
The moon is bright behind
A thick layer of clouds
That scrappily attempt to erase its light.

Streetlamps are spotlights
That force my display; those glances
I've come to embrace are diverted
By my naked forearm.
Most tender are those who hide away,
Who can relate, but from the shadows.
Their outstretched arms, veiled to me,
Are the only shelter I can find warmth in.

This storm hums in voices around my head,
Bees in a jar trying not to drown in honey
Stolen from their own combs.

Disguised as a warning, but only
An intervention meant to rattle my own roots.
Little do I know: the soil loosens beneath me.

IV

Lightning strikes circles around me,
Symbols that crash and block out any other sound.
My ears ring, a deafness, a language barrier
Between me and those who only think in binaries,
Who chose when they reached the fork in the road
Instead of hacking at the brush straight ahead.

These gusts now threaten to stagger my steps,
Knock the wind from my lungs,
Quiet my voice.
This is not a stumble, but a dance,
Headfirst into the forest for the trees,
Where tattered, tri-colored flags
Hang from damp branches.
I brush my hands along the bark,
Rough but protective against
All foreign elements.

Easing weight off my legs,
I let the gale sweep me up off the ground,
Uprooted, weightless,
And carry me to the edge,
Masked as an invisible fence
For so long.

V

Those who catch my eye
No longer find it attached to a string
So I can reel it back in.
The tempest that stole my balance
Never returned it; there's no need

When the proposed dichotomy was false.
Now I know that future storms
Are for those who need to learn
To dance in the rain.

And the leaves still dance around my feet
To a much more soothing song, now that
I've shortened all of my sleeves.
Aside from never earning a perfect score,
And knowing I'll never have to,
The slipshod "A" on my skin just isn't
Noticeable enough for it to really matter,
At all.

ACKNOWLEDGEMENTS

I would like to thank everyone who helped bring this book to life: Joshua Unger, Jessica d'Arbonne, Dani Dymond, and Sarah Parke. It takes a lot to put such personal work out there in the world, and I couldn't have done it without any of you. Thanks for pushing me to embrace my vulnerability, and for telling me when my poems are bad. And thank you to Sarah Farrell for making me look great in my author photo.

Earlier versions of some of the poems in this book have been appeared in several publications: "Faulty Wiring" (Freshwater Poetry Journal, 2015), "Reassurance" (Beechwood Review, 2015), "Imperfect Fit" and "Some Things You Can't Undo" (Folio Literary Magazine, 2016), and "The Oldest Rules in the Book" (Moon Tide Press, *Dark Ink*, 2018).

ABOUT RYAN MEYER

Ryan Meyer is a Southern Connecticut State University graduate whose work has been featured in Freshwater Poetry Magazine, Beechwood Review, Folio Literary Magazine, and Moon Tide Press' *Dark Ink* Anthology. His first book of poems, *Haunt*, was self-published in February 2018. He lives in Shelton, Connecticut.

Follow Ryan at NothingPeak.com.

CPSIA information can be obtained
at www.ICGtesting.com
Printed in the USA
FSHW021950220121
77773FS